A VOICED AWAKENING

A VOICED AWAKENING

Poems

David Jaffin

First published in Great Britain in 2004 by
Shearsman Books,
58 Velwell Road, Exeter EX4 4LD
and in Germany by
St.-Johannis-Druckerei, Lahr/Schwarzwald

www.shearsman.com
shearsman@macunlimited.net

Distributed for Shearsman Books in the U.S.A. by
Small Press Distribution, 1341 Seventh Avenue, Berkeley, CA 94710
Email: orders@spdbooks.org
Website: http://www.spdbooks.org

ISBN 0-907562-57-4 (Shearsman Books, UK)
ISBN 3-501-01499-6 (St.-Johannis-Druckerei, Germany)

Gesamtherstellung: St.-Johannis-Druckerei, Lahr/Schwarzwald
Printed in Germany 34847/2004

Contents

That first snow

is more in
the tensions

releasing
now that

depth
from sky.

Of unspoken touch

That

no where
time of

now in the
fragrance

of flower'
s unspoken

touch.

Holy Communion

If

it was only
the knees

that bent
their will

under the
weight of

being too
much in

self.

At the Window's edge

Flowers

at the win-
dow's edge

Being clo

sed in to a
room of

self-told

thoughts.

The Season for War

September

not the song
of a last-

felt longing
But the season

for war
That need for

blood ri
sing to its

own account
s as these

leaves turn
for color and

the nights
take in their

cold breath
strange

ly apparent.

Planning

What

we've plann
ed isn't

what's plan
ning us

The general'
s astute

eyed-in
time-less

glanced of the
where death'

s where he
isn't Fields

of blood at
tuned from

his paper
less smile.

Paradox

If

war doesn'
t solve

but create
s new field

s in uncer
tainty There

may still be
a time

when to re
treat simply

postpones
the date of

that encounter
Man's at

war with him
self and can'

t solve what
he can't create

even in the
undoing of

himself.

Preemptive Strike

If

we attack
the danger

before It
endanger

s us as in
the writhing

of a snake'
s coiled stance

We may cut
it through to

the steel-
ed edge of

our own ex
pectation

s by doubling
the strength

of its re
coiled attack.

Hot days, cold nights

and it's
hard to keep

the balance
intact Where

the moon's
decisive

glow appro
priates more

of my person
than fears

can speak a
loud And the

afternoon'
s sun flour

ishes an a
bundance

of superflu

ous light.

Flemmish, 15th century

The pur

ity of these
Marian hymns

The clear
lines of ex

pressing
the unity of

phrasing What
we aren't

she became

for us.

Blow fish

bigger than
he felt he

could possi
bly be In

flated as
Balloon's

rounding
readi

ness.

Strange birds

wingèd with
imagined

colors Staring
out silent

repeating wa
ters.

Mother Goose rhymes (5)

*a) "Diddle, diddle
dumpling My son
John' …"*

s an on and
off sort of

poem The way
we tend to

be As if
moods could

be interchange
able with those

shoes and
day dreams

were kept for
night's sleep

ing in.

b) "There was a little
girl, she had a
little curl ..."

I don't know
at the middle

of what For
she was either

/or ing it
As the blink

ing of an
eye's nasty/

prettied look.

c) "O, the grand old
Duke of York ..."

We're still

marching our
soldiers a

round Even if
practice

can still
make Perfect

ly disconten
ed.

d) "Little Miss Muffit
sat on a puffit ..."

Sofas can still

sink us in
to those twi

light zones
of tasty

unease.

e) "The king was in
his parlour
counting out his
money ..."

A plea

surable pur
suit for those

who can af
ford it And

the honey
might taste

even sweeter
than her all-

presuming

smiles.

A lightness

These

sands co
lor the light

ness of the
sky's trans

parently

blue.

Pretty

a word for a
woman dressed

in a light-
defining

blue Rimmed
in the white

ness of where
scarcely

clouds almost
touched to

the horizon
ed edge.

Kayaks

parting the
water's edge

with a re
clining ease

for touching
those proba

bilities of
distancing

in spaced.

Making person

If

making mon
ey's making

person Why
haven't we ac

quired a pa
pered face

then.

With the deaf congregation I

All those
waving wild

ness of hand
s sig

nalled- in
sense and at-

tributes of
mind Taking on

the meaning
of what

words have fin
ally come to

imply.

Hardened

bone-felt

hand
speaks

of a life

without e
ven an eye-

touched

glimmer.

"The way I see it"

If it's

the way I see
it What hap

pens when I
can't see

anything

anymore.

With the deaf Congregation II

For

words were
for them as

the soundless
speakings of

the ocean's
depths They

heard that
they knew.

Cadences of sound

like the fal
ling of wa

ter's light
impression

ably still
ed.

Small talk

Talking

about What
one talks a

bout
Like the chat-

ter of bird
s activa

ting with
out bringing

those leave
s back to

life.

Poems about poem (2)

a) A single word

may cleanse
the meaning

of that
phrased-in

sense.

b) To reclaim language

is like
weeding a

garden from
its over

grown usage.

Late-down flowers

and their
color's fray

ed like the
cloth of

to(o)-seen
clothes

worn for ap
pearance

of that
daily smile

one's be
come too

accustomed
to(o).

Learning

One

doesn't
learn to

write One
writes by

learning

how.

Pawed

That

cat pawed
its secre

tive in
stincts to

those step
s of see

ing eyes.

Realizing

If

children's
thoughts

seem bigger
than they can

see It's be
cause they'

re/bigger

than they
them selves

Realizing.

In the quiet

It's only

in the quiet
of where

we come back
to ourselve

s that this
room's be

coming per
soned.

Awakening

Leaves

folding in
the wind a

voiced a

wakening.

Subtractions

He

denied more
of himself

than he could
find back

to.

For heavenly recline

Clouds

continuing
their own

way Shadow
ing the earth'

s moments for
heavenly re

cline.

Hardy – Return of the native (4)

a) Eustasia Vye

She was some
thing more

than person A
beauty be

yond the claim

s of what

beauty can mean

to the heath'
s ever present

thereness
being more

than what She
was or even

of that where
that couldn'

t hold her.

b) Reddleman

The

eyes that
watch over us

can be per
soned as well

Not from a
bove or even

within But at
a distance Claim

ing that near
ness for.

c) Heath people

A

part of that
whereness

superstitious
ly alive to

truths beyond
the mind's

seeing
Timeless as

the heath'
s Breeding

in that al
ways there

ness of.

d) Clym's mother and that closed door

Why

that door
was closed

Because we
can't see be

yond what has
happened A

finality of
sense A brood

ing truth as
the heath it

self Closing
us out by

Taking us in.

Card Players *(Cezanne)*

These

cards have
touched them

selves to
their fin-

gered needs
that complete

in eyed-
from certain

ties.

The poem, the way it is

Some
thing gro

wing within
myself May be

the way the
earth in

spring feels
itself coming

through to
bloom in flo-

wered color

s.

Listening

to the move

ments of his
thoughts

on this stone-
felt sur

face Upset

him as
colors

didn’t quite
match this

sense of
seeing A

slight un-
easiness

crept
through his

untried veins.

Lessened

Saying

it less is
meaning it

more And
what's un

said con
tinues to

think.

Non-Heritage

Jesus

couldn't
prove that

he wasn't
Jewish

But the
church has

often given
proof of

its non-

heritage.

Borderline

She

crouched
in defiance

of herself
The lioness

defending
what She

could only

devour.

For Ernst

Listening

may be a
part of

why the poem'
s the way

It is.

Viktor Frankl *April 1945*

To

lose all
is to know

all We need
to know.

Isaac

He

knew His
father knew

the cause
the love

the where
ness of

his being

Bound/

there to
the fear in

his help
less cries

at the stake
the fire of

God's burning
justness.

Recognition

Looking

through glass
May be the

same person
If he sees

the way
I'm seeing

him in.

Night's voices

To
the whisper

ing of moon'
s lightèd

thoughts And
those voice

s through
unanswer

ing stars.

Arm chairs

in a certi-
tude of

self-assur
ance Cir

cling last
night's con

versations
Holding in/

there

for voice.

Snails and others

maintain

a household
in self-

protective
seclusion

But man walls
himself in

to systems
of self-de

termina
tion.

Inspoken

Looking

herself
down to

her son's
telling eye

s may have
spoken her

years younger.

Incessantly so

Chatter
ed on in-

cessant
ly so Like

birds chea-
ting for

the crumbs
of lesser

pleasure
s.

Dream-for songs

My

father sang
his dream-

for-songs Trai
ling his fee

lings to

beyond
long-lost

desires.

Concealing in

Night

came
through the

slow wind
s of con

cealing in
depths of

hidden

darkness.

Nathaniel Pink: in retrospect

He was

so exact
in precising

his culti
vated ends

Taking the
meanings to

the length of
their long-

desired-in
tentions That

his world
seemed made-

over
for the glit-

tering win
ding paths

of where
those stars

could be
turned in or

out at the
ease of his

elongated

whispering
s.

Thaw

One

can only
really know

what that
soft ness

means After
the hard-

cold of con-
tracting

to the mus-
cles and

bones of our
restrain-

ed desires
Melting.

Just for a moment

the buds

of touch
ing his fin-

ger's wants

for light.

Brueghel: 2 Paintings

a) The Blind following the blind

I'm

not certain
If there

may be a
cliff hanging

down some
where that

empty
feeling in

the depths of
my hollow

ed in
thoughts.

b) The Tower of Babel

Such

heights
may blind us

to a view of
ourselves

Taking stone
instead of

the pulse
of where

flesh speak
s aloud

that stone-
touched

in death.

Concert goers

Most

were listen
ing to what

They were told
to listen for

Like catch
ing an undis

covered mouse
because the

traps were set-
in their cor

rectly baited
fashion.

Such Witnesses

All these
windows loo

king out
through their

glass-reflec-
ting eyes

Witnesses
to this speech

less void of
our blinding

times.

Whiteness of

As swans
shadow their

whiteness
in the cool

awareness
of their

passing
through these

upturned
waves.

Surprised awakenings

In

those sur
prised awaken

ings as flo
wers un

earthed
from being

kept cold
and dark so

long.

Workman

His

hands rough
ed to the

numbness
in this win-

tered cold
Spading

this half-
frozen earth

to an indel-
ible warmth

his hands
had long since

been telling.

A logic to faith?

If

there's a
logic to faith

it's because
what I think

can't think
me beyond the

bounds of my
pre-determin

ed person Love
less as such

and in the
eyes of death

helpless

as well.

The Liberal creed

believes in a
man better

ed than I've
come to know

And the pro
gress of a

progressive
ly dismal

world I'd be
a liberal

If I didn't
know myself

Better than

that!

On the Alert

alarming co-

lors melting
into a flow

of imagined
thoughts

Upsetting

whatever ba
lance I

could ease out

from there.

This last berried touch

to its har-
dened co-

lored sense
of There-I-

am regained
for this mea

ning to tell.

A Door

could go ei
ther way

But if you'
re alone

That touch of
its used-

in presence
is like Ask-

ing your
self Why you'

re coming back
to what

isn't there.

This ground's

frozen into
its times of

forgetful
ness Like some

animals who
take their win-

ter sleep in
those urging

s for a depth
of silence

quiet-
held in

that
overfelt flow

for stars.

A rabbit's Softness

i felt
into a flow

ing warmness
of why It

needed to
jump As a poem

that couldn'
t stay still

in its accept
ance of be

ing there.

Innocent continuity

This

snow's in
nocent contin

uity As if
All the world

could be told
through the

whiteness
of its alway

s coming

times.

Opened Piano

O
pened The

keys in
black for

white

running their
length to a

presuppos
ed sense for

sound.

Emptied waiting room

Rows

of seat
less person

s having
been where

they aren't
now A lone

liness of
watching spo

ken shadow
s emptied

of their
voices

through.

"Giving in to oneself"

but who's
giving and

what's re
ceiving And

are we two
selves in a

dialogue
between the

one as o
ther Or would

giving out
from be a bet-

ter method
for pleasing,

so to say,
the "real

self".

"Don't trouble trouble unless trouble troubles you"

but some
people seek

trouble by not
troubling a

bout what
could possi

bly be Unpre
pared in their

defense of
Habitual mid-

streamers
without know

ing where the
other side

might bring
them in for.

"Scatter-brained"

because

she scatter

ed her
thoughts and

doings out
beyond the

range of
bringing them

back in

again.

That "stiff upper lip"

might har-
den even those

sensitive
realms of where

a kiss could
flow into real

izing unend
ing streams

those melting

winds

through desire.

"Finding oneself"

is like
a game of

hide and seek
Wherever you

are isn't
what you're

looking for
And where

you aren't
is still to

be found

out.

Jungle-jim

But

in a jungle
You can't

get to the
heights of

Entangled
in the over

growth of
finding your

self in

for out.

Making meanings

One

word may
make the mea

ning of a
poem As

a bird ten-

tatively
grasped-in

branch even
more than it

could conceive
then.

Two ways

a) what is
isn't what

it seems
to be be

cause I
tell it in

my way And
it implie

s that other
wise sense

for being.

b) It

may not be
the way

We see
things But

how They'
re seeing

us.

A tree without leaves

naked to
the out-

lines of
its being

seen through.

Fossils

are

where me
mories can

only be
touched

from.

Carpet

woven in

to its pre
determined

design Co-
lors itself

as a man
readied in

smiles that
speak increa

singly a-

loud.

Night-time shadows

less dark
as the shade

s of previous
thoughts But

only slight
ly touched-

Awakened

in view.

In losing scent

Roses

wither-
ed to their

dryness
in losing

scent.

Advent: wisemen from afar

What

they saw in
that felt-

distance
from a cer-

tained star
through the

longings of
those fol

ding field'
s increa

sing hopes
to that mo-

ment-felt in
the nearing

light of an
eternal

truth.

Of false expectations

Some

threads can
take the

fabric out
of its in-

tended de-
signs dis-

colored from
misuse And

worn down as
the range

of these pro
mising hill

s from the
breadth of

such false
expectat

ions.

If Croce

was fat
dictatorial

and distaste
ful for all

that's seen
and heard Where

does his History
of Freedom

bring him

in.

Outgrown

my
high school

days Though
the weeds

of their en
during sense

Would have
choked this

pre-intended

bloom.

Chest of drawers ca. 1900

Wood carved
in a glass-

telling view
of a world

long since de-
ciphered

As words
written to be

privately
kept through

those touch-
telling mo

ments of a
vanishing

time.

Preparing for

what we
don't know

will be
That tense pres-

sured blood
Tight-clas-

ped-in Tim-
ed of not

yet where.

Killing Christ

They

tried to
kill him

then to(o)
That time

in the blood
of infant's

cries But now
through the

dissimula
ting word that

created Him
in the revela

tion of the

Holy Spirit.

Washed out

This

land's wash
ed out

of whatever
meaning It

could have
held through

that blood-
letting time

Soaked in the
depths of

where con
science lost

its feeling
for

in the trivi
alities of

Changing
truths

shifting mea
nings And the

High priest
of Baal's

rhythmic
urge for a

lesser self.

Holy night

It

was so quiet
in that

night That he
could almost

hear it thin
king out

through space
to where A

choir of star
s singing

in their
brightness

enchanted
his mind with

some thing
like a peace

Angelically
distanced

but yet ra
diantly

near.

Israel

Being

chosen
selected

specially
from all the

peoples of
the earth

to deny their
own heritage

that the hea
then might be

told-in the
truth of that

ever-lasting

love.

The Shepherds

the chosen

are the least
apparent

not in their
Way But in

His desire
s to touch

them in the
truth of His

explicit
ly near.

The Manger

no place
to be for one

of human-kind
They eyed His

presence An
intruder or

their creator
As human-

kind would eye
him a bit

later.

Sectarian

Only

they seemed
to know

but ex-

actly the
meaning of

God's will
and word

Dressed in
the piety of

their thor
oughly self-

satisfy
ing instinct

s.

Sectarian II

That

room had too
many closed-

in window
s about it

and their fa

ding but
still angelic

apprecia
tive smiles

As of the child-
like in their

early 80s Ex
pecting the

wings of their
own saving-

through

Grace.

Shyness

may be
a tenta

tive uncer
tainty of fee

ling in to
the where

of your own
imagining

self.

That sofa

display

ing the embro
deries of

its newly
dressed pre

sence As a middle-
aged woman

eying-in
the wherea

bouts for her
self-seem

ed sense.

"Getting down to business"

may imply
that you're

up somewhere
else and per

haps need
those circui

tous stairs
to wind your

self back
down again Or

is that laz
iness biding

your time a
way from the

busi ness
of where You

should be
down to(o).

Who's measuring who?

If

the times
are the mea-

sure of
God's word

Why did He
measure us

out through
the timeless

ness of His
knowing

wisdom.

That static landscape

standing up
to itself

as far as the

seeing its
flat-length

ed coldness

in view.

Colored rolling

Ball's co-

lored roll
ing through

the hands
of its round

edness

from.

Aron at age three

activa

ting more
than he can

keep from
quieting his

thoughts

back to.

Shutter's

closed from

their seeing
out to a

world of
darkness

prevading
eye's view.

Conceit

may lower
the estimate

to your
stuck-up

self
Where comb

ing it back
down may

not please
the delicacy

for your
finger's

grace.

Self-importance

implies that
there's a

self to be
important a

bout But he
judged other

s with the
standards

He'd set for
himself As if

those other
s were there

to answer for
what He hadn't

made known
of their un

tried wan-

tings.

Airport

Lights

set up
to stand

witness
ing in dark

The nowhere
out of here

that wasn't
there Barbed-

wired.

Downed

It rained

my memories
down Like

leaves fall
ing through

those over-
crowding
nights.

Nathaniel Pink's mid-morning

Those

beauties smi
ling back at

him to clean
his teeth

a bit harder
Shining up

for that mid-
morning's inquis

itively mir-
rored glance

for the assur
ance that

He's coming
well along for

a belated stroll
with his ne

glecting dog.

Waking from snow

its cool
light increa

sing aware
ness in that

feeling-
through- dark

of why those
stars have

out told their
last glimmer

ing sensed
for night.

Snow melting this hill down

in the phrase
s of refinding

curves and
shapes of its

shaped for.

If that's progress

we learn by
losing what

we learned
by using

But not for
an out las

ting sense.

We never know

if it's the
last time

A call that
left her dy

ing beside
that unused

bed. A house
lived in

through us
But not re

turned to
But what we

never know
may be know

ing us now.

For Rosemarie

It's

because you'
re always

there That I
can find my

way back to
what I've

always want
ed to be –

You make the
most of me.

Unleft

The

birds have
taken all

their colors
away And left

me to the
bareness of

these winter-
ing wants.

21 Oak Lane

The

whiteness
of that castle-

like-house
seemed less so

after this
light powder

ed snow had re
dressed its

cause for stan
ding still

so long.

Early morning swim

He

needed the
cool of tou

ching through
the feel

of his bo-
died claims

And that fresh-
ness of think

ing those
early morning

thoughts a-
live.

These sleepless winds

restless
with un

dreamed
thoughts

and of the
waves sear

ching for
morning'

s light.

Those palms

in the soft
ness of

their flow
ing winds

have swayed
my thought

s in sleep.

Of lasting time

Morning

and these wave
s have been

calmed
coming in as

the woven
thoughts of

lasting time.

Out at sea

Ships

far out at
sea dis

tancing me

from myself.

Living up your faith alone

may be more
yours than His

who created
you and Not

you Him in the
image of your

own devotion.

Have you ever asked

why these
roads extend

two direc
tions by claim

ing the one
or even the

other It's
like Christ'

s spreading
out His arms

so far
as that un

foreseen He
knew but

these roads
seem at time

s motionless
in their

just being

passed by.

Hunger's

the rage
of these cliff

s torn from
every self-

satisfying
view these

tourists have
tucked in their

hand- guides
Steeped down

to that fin-
alized fear

ed-in depth

s.

For our children's sake

What

ever our
parents made

of us
may have out

lasted its
meaning

for our
children'

s sake.

Freed

She smiled
her wrin-

kles free
to a child-

like meaning
an eager

ness for eyes
speaking

loud again.

Jonah and the Storm

Jonah

couldn't
sleep his

conscience
clean as

Jesus' dis
ciples in

the garden
of His fear

s We often
deny Him by

just being
the way we

are.

"He's not quite himself"

implies that
that "he's"

and that "self"
complement

each other as
one But what

of that o
ther self that

seems like whis
pering from

the shadowed
realms of other

wiseness Or
those in-bal

anced sensiti
vities that

hold to their
own way of

finding from
self out.

Holbein the Younger's "Last Supper" *(Basel)*

Nothing

on that table
was the way

It was meant
to be – Pass

over seemed
here to be

passed over
from its sym

bolic intent
And Judas slouch

ed into an
ever-presence

otherwise
ness of

"Judaic

cunning".

Country dining with Ingo and Solvay

Somewhere

from that near
ness of Ven

etian over-
present price

s And those
refuged shadow

s that still
plague from its

past Here in the
country side

where breathing
really takes

the air in
And taste is

opulently
enchanced

from view.

Of re-seeming eyes

Watching

little crea
tures in the

wood with the
respecta

bility of re-
seeming eye

s our own
inner notion

s of word

in sense.

Romanesque

Thicken

ed protective
walls Assum

ing a lesser
height for

closed-
in prayers

to the dark
of an in-

revealing God
surrounding

himself with
penitant de

votions.

Up stream

As

fish swee
ping the cur-

rents with
their flash-

for-scaling
fins He tried

to force him
self against

those inner
tides to his

improbably
found-for

self.

Low tide

That

long flat
tened line

of beached-
in steps Calm

ing the wave
s in to that

smoothed sur
face

evening out
the length to

my own clear
ing through

thought

s.

Sea-side houses

These

houses
framed to

the voice of
the sea's

listening
to their loo

king out Con
stantly ap

pearing.

Train stops

starting

again after
the signals

have changed
As if that

train hadn't
all along

been taking
its stations

in Albany
New York in

that night-
glassed image

of seeing my
child's eye

s through the
windows of that

unseen dark'
s not reali

zing myself

from where.

Outlasted

That

house out
lasted its

time Where
others moved

we stayed
When others

would have
built anew

That house re
peated its wan

ting claims on
becoming

through us
Am I (then)

that house
that didn't re

main?

Can you familiarize stone

by looking a
cross the lake

to those dis-
tance-seen

cities Where
the hills glad

ly take them
up embracing

time in place.

Moving on

This

lake's moving
on as a guide

book for kno
wing where But

with the wind'
s transparent

meanings and
where swans re

creating through
their whiteness

that silent
flow from be

ing there.

At 65

there's more
of sleep

becoming of
me Cocooned

in a closed-
in-silence

of butter
fly's

dreams.

Ice-cream man

changed song
But not fla

vours Always
the same re

peating them
that he sleep

s to the taste
of the sound'

s flavour.

Than this

It

can't get
much colder

than this
down here

where Florida'
s buried in

the heat of
warmed up de

sires And
winds chilled

by evening

thoughts.

Dolphins

presuming
another sense

of world
Between sea

and air see
king out

that language
for words.

Blue Marlin'

s sanctity
in color

Only the sea
can tell

the streaming
length of its

callings and
the plungings

of its deepen
ing finds.

Pre-established presence

At the top

of these pole'
s pre-estab

lished pre
sence of birds

staring out
their unseen

in-knowing

stillness.

Osprey

Too big fish
might weigh

them down
So they must

choose their
appetites

for somewhat
smaller ta

kings As a
modest poet'

s for just
the rightly

weighted

words.

Can we tame the sea

manicured
in that touch

of shell
with domesti

cating sails
Whitening

its expanse
with our own

pleasuring
needs Fished

down to the
bottom of where

these appetite
s dwell.

Sand Piper's

smallness
in quicken-

ing feet's
touching

the surfac
ed imprint-

ing moment'
s needs.

Australian pines

rising

me up to
their shaded

height's
growth from

silenced

sway.

Dead pelican

head

buried in the
sand from

the heights
of his climb

ing wings and
gliding sha

dows surveying
for fish tee

ming in their
surfaced glance

Now head's
turned in

that shallow
reach for

sand.

What man means by freedom

as the square
ness of that

pool defining
in the even-

armed of those
stroking

lengths a cer
tained and

guaranteed
course of

self- dir
ection.

Curls

The

curls of his
hair indis

tinguished
from less-

oriented
thought

s Hanging loose
sun-glassed

perspec
tives.

When her grandmother died

the one whose
heart was

bigger than
the place where

It was meant
to be The flo

wers were
crying And

that little
girl almost

6 or 7 lost
more of her

self than any
little ness

could pos
sibly have

known.

Writing myself wake

in the in
delible

ink of
person and

page.

Seeing it straight

as an arrow
Quivered

in its mark.

Starting a poem'

s like beginn
ing yourself

All over a
gain.

"Felt it that way"

You may have
felt it

that way But
does the

page reveal
the same.

Criminals

If

you don't let
them be pu-

nished They'
ll punish

you more with
their unre

solved guilt.

A strange bird

not yet map
ped out to

my sense of
name Appearing

to a nearness
of finding

me something

more.

Because he wasn't flying

that small
blue heron's

thinness in
feet Angled

an uncertain
impression

from place.

What secrets

have these
sands buried

deeper than
the knowing it

can tell These
broken hopes

as shells wash
ed up from

their dried-
down claim

s.

Morning streetlights

as if the
dark was still

turned on
Breeding an

unseen fear
Reaching

through those
silent depth

s for night.

The slightness of this pen

can only
touch the out

lines of what
I'm meaning

for.

This blue shell

ringed with
the circles It

couldn't con
tain A round

ness that told
for the sea'

s voice per
fectly still

ed.

Helen's romantic urge *(in Howards End)*

to fulfill
her self- deny

ing self The
way flower

s deem their
light for a

desert

setting.

Border states

All

states border
on others

or a state of
mind that

can't quite
place its

whereabouts

from.

Self-imaged

To believe

in God's be
lieving in

you isn't al
ways the

same.

Horseshoes

aimed

with the eye
or hands

tightly
taught to

find in spac
ed between.

Mr. Wilcocks *(in Howards End)*

To

own up to
what will find

you out The
hide and

seek of life'
s perform

ing game.

Handyman

Whatever

went wrong
He fixed it

back to place
Agile with

hands eye-
minded/de-

tailed But his
life was

out of
place Couldn'

t come to grip
s to where

His
eyes seemed

helpless
ly insecure.

The Basses *(in Howards End)*

She

caged him
in As a parrot

celebrating
colors She

fed with her
eyes and bo

died kept
in.

Phil

He had a

trucker's
strength but

mild hands
toned down

voice
quick to a

word glimmer-
ing his eyes

into eager-
ed presence.

Tempting a smile

in that shy
ness of an

incomplet
ed self-

sense As if
touch could

signify its
own rights

Brighten
ing you in

to that mir
rored glance.

Falling with Snow

These

mountains
falling with

snow the
last impres

sions from
their winter'

s weighted

silence.

Taking a Measure by myself *(Hommage à Wordsworth)*

I've sat
under this same

tree 30 odd
years now

with much of
myself be

tween As this
lake measur

ing out the
distance to

where these
trees comb the

otherside in
And the same

birds or re
lated off

spring retell
ing their mea

ning for con
tinuing song

That time melt
s rather than

measuring in
to my sitting

myself out

once again.

Becoming aware

is like
those colors

coloring
me Or the hesi-

tant pull of
shadows

inside/from.

Melting down

This

snow's fa
ding out

Melting sha
dows down

to those
deep tree-

lines dark
ly exposed con

tinuing

growth.

Spitzweg: Hunter in the Woods

Why

did that deer
happen to

happen Right
there with

his al
most smiling ar

ticulation
When the hun

ter's mouth
stuffed with

the sausaged
taste of wood

ly enclosure
s And the nec

essary wine
to finish off

the length of
such pro

ceedings.

Spitzweg: The Butterfly Chaser

It couldn'

t possibly
be that big

His eyes bul
ging with wing

èd intent
But this net

smaller than
the confines

of his irretrie
able hopes

That the butter
fly stood con

templating
for a long while

the indigenous
designs of

his own secur
ing leisure.

"Pouring one's heart out"

The problem

with pouring
one's heart

out is that
even those rein-

forced damns
might break-

through with
too much

flooding.

Your collared suit

but

newly starch-
ed in with

reinforced

conclusions.

Narrowed

That squirrel

the one
in black

narrowing
the branch

to his slender
ness of feet-

finding.

Through emptied branches

a bird sings
flowing songs

Awakening

greeness
through those

unfolding

leaves.

Perspectived

He

was told
from various

sides As a
tailor pin-

ning down for
performance.

Dream-felt

Houses

passing
through me

mories of
having been

trans
parencies

in thought

dream-felt.

Soundless voice

Crystall

ed sha
dows snow-

flaked sound
less voice.

Only the outside now

You're

only the out
side now for

my having been
there White co

lumned to those
pre-establish

ed heights
in holding me

up from the
red brick bright

ening my return
s into those

interior claims
drawing me

through a close
ness of that

familiarly
known's only

the outside now
passing me by

unredeemed hope
s of your long

forgotten
claims on my

having been
there in leav

ing you now
as in then.

This wording of

Have

the times
changed this

wording of
Or do we

sense and
feel the same

but need fresh
claims in the

retelling for.

Borderline

He was

there for Be
wildering

the inside
out of others

Until that car
hit him down

to those be
wildering

pains through
his self's

meaning.

Winding a clock

up to im-
pulsing his

hands with
life-like.

Would/would??

If

she stood up
to his ta-

king her down
Fist-minded

pains Would he
be smaller

still Backing
off frighten-

ed through her
woman's deter

mining stance
Or would he

hit her down
again through

those freely-
found instinct

s from the
strength of

prisoning
walls.

Murky persons

inhabiting
the lower le

vels as in the
sea depth's

dark of where
light's re

fracted from
its clarify

ing/glan
ced.

Of secret, untold meanings

Carrying

down to the
sea The

gleam of
these Venctian

palaces'
unspoken

truths
cleansed of

fears and
Their secret

untold mean

ings.

Enthroned Madonna and Saints

(Bellini, 1505, S. Zaccaria)

As if

there's
nothing left

to be said
in this im

movable
perfection

of person
and place

The harmonies
of color

and sound a-
live to that

stillness
of always be

ing there.

Afterall

Spring

may afterall
only be

flowered
because

there's more
lightness

of mind.

Like other ships

Friend

ship's
like other

ships Sail
ing an un-

certain
course Some

times quic-
kened for

wind or les
sened in

that lei
sured

for seeking
more If there'

s a harbour
here then

Why are the
anchors so

short to

reach.

Too white

These walls
too white

to be tell
ing anything

new.

Broken out nut-shell

as if
words could

only live
when not

fully ex

posed.

Listening

for the
sounds of

flowers

growing.

Taking leave

Funerals'

a ta
king leave

not of the
dead But of

our living
memories

of where He
could be

told back

from.

A thirst for words

There's

a thirst
for words

Like
the need for

splitting
wood to that

coldness
of fore-

telling

hands.

Rowers *for Ingo*

The rough-
ness of that

wood could
only be mea-

sured to
their ensu-

ring hands-
of Boats gli

ding past
all expecta

tions.

Unquiets

We are

all those
who read us

in differ
ing ways

The poem un
quiets

in its

stilled-from

presence.

Strung

Those
rain-beads

budding in
their last-

told message
as the pur-

ity of pearl
strung

from its
self-enclos

ed meaning.

Displayed-in item

He

was so fas-
tidious

ly groomed
to a cele

brated appear
ance That

it was like
china not

to be touch
ed or even

turned a
bout

those phases
illumina

ting light
But just

there to be
seen as a

permanent
ly display

ed-in item.

Nathaniel Pink on the world situation

This

world may
be turning a

bout in its
pre-described

fashions un-
settling all

that ease of
my warm-

bathed inclu-
sions – Did

you hear it
then, there,

or any
where Now

Coloring my
semantic

thoughts
That little

ness of bird
just fit

for its dis-
cerning

moment.

Dresden: 5 paintings

a) Cranach: Paradise

What

God created
for man

took his
own way out

leaving those
animals all

alone to
people his

forelorn

hopes.

b) Cranach: Fall of Man

Equal

rights
for Adam

His own fruit
ed touch

ed the naked
ness of

death's loom
ing call.

c) Titian: Paying taxes to Caesar

You

can divide
a coin

that way
The Emperor'

s godly per
manence

more than
touching the

surface
to Jesus'

undivided re
ply.

d/e) Rembrandt's Saskia and Rubens Portrait of a lady

There's

a beauty of
the flesh

so sensu
ously recrea

ting in that
deepening

teint for
color And the

glowing-gold
of her hair'

s spelled-
in promise

But there's
also a beauty

beyond defin
ing itself

in her ligh-
ted eyes

to some
thing more

than just
seeing there.

Child's eyes

He

sees me
bigger than

I am
What I know

he knows
more by not

knowing yet
the open

color of his
eyes re

colors my
sense for see

ing so.

Wheel-chaired

to her help
less fin

ding feet'
s Eyes rest

lessly a
bandoned their

permanent
ly ground-

place.

Angelic

"Getting
out of hand"

may imply
that your

feet aren'
t always on

the ground.

Our background

keeps get
ting to the

forefront
of our reali

zing in
now.

After glow

When

color
melts in

to sound
And the stone'

s bright
with moon'

s after

glow.

"Thinking positively"

may negate
more of

what thin
king's

all about.

Free

to do and
saying en-

tangled with
in his sha

dowed-for

self.

Over voiced

That

music over
voiced his

trying to
listen

in.

Unsettled

It's be

cause of
these small

changes that
often un-

settle us
The older we

become The
more aware of

our body's need
s It's like

noticing a
bird for the

first time
Exactly where

it sits E
ven the ex

tent of its
song The co

loring of
its being

there And when
it starts

to fly That'
s where

We're most un-
certain for

our own ba-
lancing mea-

sure of

things.

Passah Haggadah *(Passover)*

It

may be that
This day is

like any o
ther day

But asking
it anew may

change the
certitude of

its being
there

It's the

asking it that
matters Not

that day at
all Freedom'

s the aware
ness of time'

s changing
And that's

where God
fulfills the

meaning of

himself.

Plain talk's

the mid-
western e

vener Not
where moun

tains or even
hills acquire

a beyond-it

of a certain
sameness

where even
these flowing

fields wind-
bound to the

breadth of un
defined

spaced one
ness

that plain

ness

for speech.

Obscuring

These

nights ob
scuring

where I can
find my

self

back to.

At the Psychoanalysts

Dr. W.

sat listen
ing.

Dr. W.
longer than
his look
could appear
sedately self-
encompassing
sat listen
ing.

Dr. W.
attempting
a smile that
could quite
break out
from the ser
iousness of
the situation

arose The way
Gluck's heroes
do in a semi-
operatic sit
uation.

Self-defining

She

cut out
the odds and

ends of
making those

flowers
look pretty

again.

Caroline

Face

puppet-round
voice a shal

lowed sweet
ness She wore

half-bright
ened color

s and fear
ed the depth

s in dark
ness Child-

like or child
ish her 46

year old
worn-from

keeping

smile.

"Baldunug Grien's Crucifixion" *(Basel)*

As if

Jesus' side
was only

pierced
through for

Thomas to
feel to the

wounds of
his own self-

wanting

spirit.

Awakening

Spring

may have
brightened

his voice
from a sha

dowless

dream.

Cross-word puzzles

may have
crossed his

mind's sha
dowing con

templa

tions.

Illmensee's

combed
through the

wave-length
of her re

ticent ducks
And a slight

wind surfacing the an-

xieties of
these uncertain

times Wind en
closed Woods

beheld The
Easter time's

blessing

from light.

Rembrandt's "Resurrection" (Munich)

Jesus

sitting off
the sleep

He knew was
more than

death And the
Angel of the

Lord light-
bound that emp

tiness of
those rock's

encompassing

claims.

On the Way to Emmaus

Have we

taken that
road to(o)

Telling the
Lord what He

didn't know
of His own

salvation
Roads can be

dark and un
certain And

we enlighten
ed with the

certainties
of our own

self-justi
fied meaning

s.

Painting over

gave her a
feeling of

freshened
cleanness

as of clothes
hanging dry

in the indel-
ible sun.

Waking through dream

as if the
sea's envel

oping a tide
less forget

fulness sur

rounded in
self as a

forelorn boat
without a

guiding star

to find.

Of promising colors

It

rained
All my ex

pectation
s away And

those fears
that tension

s find And
left a rain-

bowed ring a
bout of pro

mising co

lors.

Of untold meanings

The

way you look
ed beyond

yourself as

waves shifting
through the

tides of un
told mea

nings.

In colored

It

rained so
slightly

that you
could still

hear the in
tentions of

butterfly
wings and that

after-view in

colored.

"Justitia"

She

claimed a
self-assur

ance
High to its

non-beautified
final callings

She taught
bound through

the stature
of self-

certainty.

Neil

I found
you back a

gain Where
ever you

were is be
ing retold

for now.

Piano Lesson's

a French im
provising

theme
for those

eyed-in
touching

where

sounds.

Nathaniel Pink unearthed

That ripened
smell of some

what cloister
ed flowers un

earthed some
of his finest

feelings so
much that his

finger's
branched out

to that ne
cessity

of performing
in leafless

dance.

Overwording

If

it can't be
put down to

to where
down is Then

over wording'
s like an

gelic a

floats.

Prettiness

may pretend
to decorate

what shouldn'
t be touch

ed dee
per As a

woman orna
mented in the

cold stones
of their na

tural light.

Sleep

wakes me a
light Candles

of impercep
tible quie

tude as waves
woven in

to a time
less shore.

Beautifying

Flowers

may attract
bees to their

love-find
nectar Just by

beautifying
in their pre-

established

presence.

The example

believers
should set is

of our lost
soul The wan

derings of a
vacant mind

As of Abraham
through

those desert
s of yet

unreclaimed

land.

For my dead father, in dialogue

I knew

you knew
the stirring

of our blood'
s needs for

an indetermin
ed there

Was it that
driving unease

from our ghet
toed past

or The Lord's
unrelinguished

ed claims for
finding us

home.

Something to hide

We

all have some
thing to hide

Most always
from our

self and if
the Neighbour

s know it's
coming closer

edging in on
us Hide and

seek's life'
s game of un

founded mea
nings.

The Holy of holies

or that fruit
beyond man's

reach which we
took for death'

s pleading
call's God's

way of telling
us the un

told mysteries
He's reclaim

ed for our
beyond reach.

Trying to be humane's

a pulling a
gainst man'

s evil nature
And if he

pulls too fast
too far

there may be
little of

himself left
for helping.

Saddam's palaces

gleamed in
the gold of

his sun-
set smiles

And the dark
of those tor-

ture chamber'
s deep in the

depth of his
unfathomed

will for power
in ruins now

Classically-
cat-oriented

that ancient
culture robbed

of the ar-
tifacts of

what's past

passed.

Making us mild

Some

days make
us mild Like

that innocent
look of child-

like uncer
tainty whether

it's I or it's
breezy

light's

prevading.

Roller-Coaster

Even

if its lan
guage may

slip from
our grasp to

those rising
stars over

heard in plun
ging feeling

s of where
we aren't

returning
round for.

Mozart's Flute

running
through where

birds disperse
in awareness

azur the

of contem
plating in

water's

stillness.

Figurative houses

climbing
from pre-estab

lished hills
to a finished

stance of
gathering-in

familiar

ity.

Iraq or that Humpty-Dumpty syndrom

Taking

the language
a part's only

a part of put
ting it back

together a
gain It's that

Humpty-Dumpty
syndrom that

poets can per
form While mili

tary means
have mostly

failed.

For the ordering of things

If

The Lord cre
ated chaos

for the order
ing of thing

s to becom
ing They're

might be a
slight glimpse

of that left
for my teen

age daughter.

Schwabian Alb *for H. E.*

What

kind of
massive sleep

have you a
toned-through

This waiting
brooding si

lence Rock-
held Trees-

thought in
Climbing the

reverence
of what's past

by being

overheard.

Isaac

Son

of your father
Father of

your son That
transitional

nature of
man's non-

selective

meaning.

Meditations on Vermeer

She

may have pla
ced the ob

jects of her
world in just

the way She
saw and touch

ed them
But if o

thers did like
wise It may

not have been
her world

anymore.

22 Oak Lane

No go

ing back
The

house of
those first

seeings out
and knowings

somewhere
deep

Sold to stran

gers as if
It could be

taken away
from my gar

dened hopes
and where the

sky still re
mains in sum

mered view.

That bird

would have
died in the

thicket of
its hopeless

pleading
cries If its

voice wasn't
lifted through

those saving
hands to the

in-felt warm
th of re

gaining flight.

Birch-felt

The fineness
of these

leaves birch-
felt in moun

tain's protec
tive shadow

ings.

These bells

through

solemned
clouds

shining out
sun-told.

Samuel

quick-

faced child
Explicit

ly blond
As the shar-

pened con-
tours of re-

fining rock'
s certain

ed edge.

Grammar

is mine
to express

not its laws
But in the

expressive
ness of i-

mage crea
tings.

Outgrown

She out

grew herself
into the

shadows
of seclu

ded silence.

Until the Fox came

She was

as helpless
as that much-

loved furried
rabbit Caged

in the satis
factions

of an ordinary
life His mun-

chings on car
rots and salads

much as her
distribution

of finding
friends to keep

her in from
finding out her

helpless lone
liness Until

one night The
Fox came His

eyes staring
as the moon's

brightening
glow His jewell-

in-teeth Broke
the wirings

that held her
in that help

lessness She
couldn't get

out from.

Milkweed

floating
an occas

ional sound-
lift.

Held fast

It's

your beauty
that holds

me fast
Despite wea

kenings in
an aging

heart.

If

a butterfly
could straigh

ten its
thoughts out

It wouldn't
be as humane

as we are.

Rivered

He read

himself
through the

river's tee
ming chances

of stone-
bred light-

ning caus-
ed.

Self-Protective

Most

women want
to be cloth

ed to a na
kedness from

themselves
The liturgi

cal church
wrapped in its

own self-pro
tective

tradition
s.

Rained away

It

rained that
heat away

to a cool
ness of

somewhat
self-content

ment.

Directionless

These

tracks may
be running

still But the
trains don'

t come direct
ionless like

intently wait
ing for news

that's already
past happen

ing.

Dart game

He

threw dart
s to count

his points
to their

needled in-
sistent hand

s quiver-
ing in length.

So many doors

that he
couldn't find

the where of
finding out

the coming
back in

to.

No one to know

living in
that room

where the
clock never

theless tur
ning its

time around in
visibly de

ciphered.

The Trenches *(World War I)*

Dug

in to the
depths of

time-number
ed deaths

imperson
ally await

ing.

"To make the most of it"

implies
that the most

isn't most
ly what we're

making it
for.

That piano

reverent
ly polished

to those in

toned en
closures of

self-suffi
cient

stillness.

Candles

burned down
to their co

loring length
Renewing in

formed-re
flection.

A part of her

He

was a part
of her

being her
self As an

outer face
from being

confined

within.

Adam stripe bass fishing

This

mid-night
flood of

tide's moon-
eclipsing

their striped
through run-

gleaming-

fast.

So lived in

That room

was so lived
in That it

stopped spea
king for

itself.

Aloneness

He

inhabited
himself

in that
room of still

ed but dis
tant

houses.

Lesser Mark

Trying

to impress o
thers may

have left a
lesser mark

on himself.

Sylvia's way

Butter

flies flut
tering in

their ribbon
ed estua

ries Landing
in on

sounds.

Leafed

This

green of
having been

finally form
ed for wind'

s chanced-
through

pleasures.

Of darkening

Pulling

the shade
s down'

s another
way of darken

ing your own
sense for

night's self
enclosing

claims.

Scented

Rose

s darken
ing in the

rain Leaves
spreading

out that
scent of fal

len shadow
s.

Out blossomed

That

tree out
blossomed

itself to a
fragrance

in being

heard.

Bigger

That

car was
bigger than

she could
find of her

self sit

ting in.

After rain

there's a
fragrance

to touch
and the quiet

of moon-
spell time.

5 Masterpieces in the Alte Pinakothek, Munich

a) Resurrected Christ (Rembrandt)

Lonely

sitting
through that

waiting corner
of death'

s reviving
to the light

of the Lord'
s angelic

callings.

b) Wedding Portrait (Rubens)

You

dressed her
all up to

that shining
splendour

of a pose
Your poetic

love-felt de
sires could

only seem-
in telling as

Her touching
hand from

yours.

c) Annunciation (Bouts)

That clo

sed book
kept more of

my eyes than
what that annunci

ating angel
and Mary could

commune of an
unopened my

stery together
ed in-told.

d) Vanity (Titian)

Her

beauty held-
in more

of your self-
admiration

than even
those jewels

could mirror
through a

timeless

truth.

e) Self-Portrait (Dürer as Christ)

Those

Four Apostels e
pically I

talianite a
cross the way

from your in-
tense longing

to face in-
to Christ's fea

tures of
timeless

beauty.

A Pastel Afternoon

with fee
lings muted

in the soft
ness of not

even thinking
the why

or wherefore
of.

At the Proms

two dogs

Boston bull
black flec

ked in-
stepped a

wareness
Sequenced

their approa
ching feet.

Of marbled stone

The

cold touch
of this mar-

bled stone
permea

ting sight
through

transpar
ent vein

s Awaken
ing joy!

Historical length

These

times over
reaching

themselves
into a now

of only just
realizing

that then.

Could mean

Thinking

flowers
smaller than

the speaking
of touch

could mean.

Black Cat

in garden'
s staring

my eyes in
to its strange

ness seeing

through.

Its sense from darkness

Bird's co
lored song

in-tuned from
the wood'

s awaken
ing through

its sense
for dark

ness.

A quiet place

where wa
ters reflec

ting in the
stillness

of trans
parent

thoughts.

With Corot

This in

tending blue
cloud-

touched the
nearness of

distance
s time

lessly ap

parent.

Mass graves

That un

seen hate
Wild fears

shot into
the blood

realizing
death's un

buried from
their time

less grave

s.

Hate

screams
impassion

ed shadow

s.

Out spreading

Sha

dows spread
ing this

summer gar
den's depth

in silenced

through.

Swing

suspend
ed to the

height of ba
lancing-

in timed
aware

ness.

Cocktail Party

If

everyone'
s out to

impress

the impress
ion that's

left –

Floating

shadows.

Dream conscious

If

this climate
changes our

attitudes
That heat and

sun perpetu
ate their las

ting caused
shadow less

dream

conscious.

Chagalls "The desparate Job"

He's

bigger than
his problems

could make
him out to

be Self-im
posed The

weight of
relentless

ly untold.

Nathaniel Pink untangled

You

were more than
what was sit

ting there
Fashioned in

that pliant chair
of self-as

suming comfort
s Nat, let's

up it with me
as butterfly's

secret ways in
changing color

s You might have
been caught

through a tan-
gle of less-

prescribing

nets.

Van der Weyden's "Annunciation" *(Munich)*

Her

fear from
hand withheld

But the way
she said yes

as the cloth
of her fine

ly-told dress
touched to

that of the
angel's where

her purity-
white in the

lily enclos
sed seemed just

quite right.

After rain

and we
sensed our

selves nearer
to where

touch could
mean the sha

dow of a
glance and

that cool
light reflec

ting in-jewell
ed through.

On Shostakovich Preludes and Fugues *op 87*

If

there's a
range to be

ing left a
lone to in-

tone your own
whereabout

s through
No public

No protests
but only the

keys of dif
ferenti

ated in-touch
ed dwelling

there Soun
ded out by

hearing in.

Tolerance

is because
However much

I know
to believe

knows more
than my

knowing it.

If

there's no
longing left

That need
to be more

of what
one wasn't

The world'
s lost its

shadowing

s in.

A Form of presence

Light'

s a form
of presence

Performing
these trees

into a spo
ken awareness

of being
formed from

leafed-in'
s awaiting.

Muted now

Don't

speak too
loud now of

the dead
Because their

presence'
s muted now

through
lifeless a

wareness.

Flowered

Have

you been
flowered by

being dress
ed Awaken

ing through
in scent

for color.

Familiarity

The older

one is The
more familiar

ity recognize
s our aging-

through need
s. It might

be the lesser
self that

deeds it so
Or because

our times are
failing out.

Bach dancing

to the tune
s of his rhy

thmic free-spell
ing Impulsed

that slender
ness of less

weighted
thoughts for

merly column
ed in the

strength of
when The Lord

might defend
His chosen

in need.

Master of himself

If

man's the
master of him

self Why isn'
t he more

of what
he isn't.

Bach

may have
built on pre-

establish
ed forms

to hold their
meanings in

Castled
thorough

ly equipped a
gainst those

winds in wea
thering

times.

To be pleased's

the way lips
assume in

smile And eye
s have told

through in
finishing

form.

Through never more *(variations on a Goethian theme)*

Butter

flies over
water's reflec

ting glance
d them in

to that tide
less sway

ed through
never

more.

Nathaniel Pink's exposures

If

you can't but-
ton your

shirt in ei
ther direction

And those co
lors may not

even match to
correct

able proce
dures Why

bring your
sensibili

ties into play
like Hilary Clin

ton's autobio
graphing her

make-for

tears.

4 Squared

My glass-fram-
ed desk

adhering
its cut-from

spaced de-

fining.

Revolving doors

While

the going in
s a going

out And he
couldn't cen

ter himself
to a balanced

thereness
As if the

world was
rounded to

circling
spheres cosmi

cally rede

fining.

Solemned

This

heat weighs
heavy upon

my thought
s The clouds

closing in
to a timeless

ly now Even
the trees

breathing down
immovably

solemned.

After taste

Has

this grass
been cut to

my instinct
for light and

left a refresh
ingly after

taste as that
lightness

of butter
fly's random

ly rehears

ings.

Because

If

there's a
weight to

shadow It'
s because I'

m sitting so
heavily

now.

A white horse in a green field

flowing
through the

grace of
where He's

standing to
the beauty of

his timely

statured.

Seamed

Moun

tains skirting
their rimm-

ed-find dis
tances as the

seam of a
dressed- in

awareness
This immobil

ity for place.

Macbeth – Anatomy of a happy marriage

One heart
one soul

one hand
Their works fur

thered by a
common goal

What marriage
could equal this

for such a u
nity of purpose

They strived be
yond their weak

ness to that
daring goal In

life as in
death a oneness

our Stratfordian
bard has told

so picturesque
ly unfolding

the details of
their common

mould.

Macbeth at Burnham Woods

These

woods closing
in on me En

compassing
the depths of

such a telling
darkness The

fears of a death
I told to un

certain hands
and heart coming

back at me to
the beats of

their drums sa
tisfying in

claims against
my failing

works.

Hamlet's Stagefright

was that common
cause that kept

him from doing
the works his

father's death
demanded of

his tenderness
of mind and

mostly frigh
tened soul

That fear of
standing to

the facts Out
right upon a

stage higher
than his fear

ing feet
would climb.

Erasing memories

is like
walking on

sand in
the falling

of rain's

telling.

Of what isn't mine

Living

the room of
what isn't

mine left
after death

in being Dia
logued be

yond my sense
for seeing

speaks imperson
ally untold.

Colored carpets

uplifting
why the loo

king down'
s can't re

main

for place.

Lee's house

An

aesthetic
of light

in glassed-
through space-

defining that
outer glance

in garden.

An awayness

There

was an a
wayness of

his trying
to tell me

for true

Hand-look
somewhere a

side from
his glanced-

inward tell

ing eyes.

Horse and Rider

The

horse Carr
ying his pride

upon a hand-
topped hat

And the trott
ing echo of

feet assem
bling the thum

ping sounds
of pre-estab

lished heart

beats.

With the speed of listening by

This

train with
the speed of

listening
by as stars

flourishing
to the time-

turning of
heaven's in

volving

heights.

Agèd with the faith

tiredly
worn from

fingered-
down prayer

books The
pulse in an

other life
vaguely

touched
through in

meaning.

In rhythmic variations

This

bird's song
repeated in

rhythmic var
iations

might be a
way of re

minding him
self of what

he's remind
ing him

self for.

Beethoven Quartet op 59 No. 2

Was it that ten-
sion Or space-

creating form
Or a Shakespear

ian self-told
dialogue But

controlled to
where mea

nings stand
straight to

their being
permanent

ly upheld.

Mendelssohn Quartet op 12

(1st Mvt. first and recurring theme)

An inner

sadness trans
parently

withheld but
repeating

in almost whis
pering need

s As if tou
ching through

to that some
where from

your distan
cing self.

A fly

It

isn't what
it is But

what we've ta
ken it to

mean to be
It sits there

windowed
for a light

exposing my
view of where

I see it less
than what

it’s sensing

out.

Insisting

These

rains keep
coming down

Insisting on
whatcver

they keep tell
ing for Like

some persons
getting more

out of them
selves than we

would want to
be taking

in.

Thoughts On Sophocle's Oedipus Rex (6)

a) If the blind
know

because
we're blind in

our own see
ing out See

ing is the be
lieving in

what we can
only know

less of.

b) Seeing-eye dog

Can I (then)
scent his

world for the
length of

my own.

c) If the God's

have pre-conceiv
ed And I

am only what
they knew more

of Then why
have these Greeks made

their own un
fathomed Gods

into what is
so humanly

formed.

d) The Greek "fates" a Christian answer

Faith
love and hope

have outgather
ed All the pre

conceiveness
of my not be

ing more than
the I

I was told
to mean.

e) If Christ's

the before
knowing of All

that's Follow
ing Him is

the where I'
m not for mine

lessening

in step.

f) Too long ending

Why not

end it where
it should

without such
pathos

Pain speak
s more in its

saying less.

5 Masterpieces in Berlin

a) Guardi

That al

most unreal
faceless

world where
only light

consumes the
image of its

coming through
Waves rest

lessly uncer
tained/Sensed.

b) Canaletto

As if

Venice wasn't
floating upon

the waves of a
dreamed-

through sur
face You es-

tablished co
lumns of self-

assuring
heights and the

respect in mean
ingful archi

tectural claim

s.

c) Cranach's Fall of man

Who wasn'
t was it the

snake's whis
per or that

overbrooding
height of his

cosmic urge
for 2 fruits

2 deaths
through the

taste of their
wanting for

more.

d) e) Vermeer and DeHooch

facing each
other though

Telling in op
posite direc

tions The one
clarifying in

light the ob
jects for

touching her
personed-

through The o
ther where

door and win
dows leading

out to a space
lessness in

All consuming
light-timed.

Numbered

His

house num
bered to his

seeing in
there As if

such a sign
could relate

to where
Steps irrever

sibly stand.

Quieted down

Age

should have
quieted him

down to that
pillowed clo

sure in rest
Or where bird

s circling
in winds of

timeless
ly passed.

Baldung Grien's Crucifixion

You always

had another way
with it/Cross-

barked to where
It split at His

imploring
feet's e

longating the
weeping Maria'

s sense of our
timeless

ly told-for

sadness.

Cynthia

She

never grew
out of her

little girl'
s tears Self-

pitying why
she hadn't been

loved for more
of her own

forsaken
self.

Chagall's Crucifixions

As if

It was only
we He died

for Flesh of
His flesh

Bone of his
not being

able to be
broken through

Paschal Lamb'
s freeing

in-pained.

"Fated"?

He

couldn't help
being what

he was
helplessly

more of.

Chagall's Jeremia

Clothed

for those
blacked-in

tears Stone
formed to re

place that
broken-down

temple He sat
the ageless

ness of Israel'
s suffering

calls.

Words

are too many
of them

selves Like
these plural

ities of fish
Minnowing

to surface
claims Silver-

sensed.

Diplomatically cool

the clothes
for indecis

ive words
Those double-

meanings in
stinctive

ly formed to
that lipped-

in presence of
implied com

munication
s.

Where/who

Do

I sleep in
the night

Or does that
night sleep

through me
in the darken

ing waves en
compassing

And silence
that keeps

speaking back
into sound

less words

of dream.

Continuing on

Period

s may seek
out their

own ending
s But the

sense of
this continu

ing on.

Rising above

But

there would
be a voice

Rising above
that other

wise of lis
tening down

Where
shells out

spoken now
Conformed to

sand And those
gulls repea

ting their sha
dows of lost

moments in
the returning

seas but Now
shallowed for

touch.

For Rosemarie in Dallas, Texas

When

you aren't
there I can't

fill that space

with poem.

Looking old's

a question
of attitude

Time takes
its full if we

let it wrin-
kle us in to

a submission
of You take

I'm taken
as flowers

withered
from being

looked at
to(o) much.

So hard

He

pressed
the point so

hard 'til
it broke

off.

Trusting

Why

we trust o
thers is

because We
can't quite

find the
same in our

selves.

Open Spaces *after a 14th century Chinese master*

etched-

in to that
fineness

of detailed
design

What could
n't be answer

ed Listening

out.

"Reality therapy"

He de-

tailed his own
sense for that

being here for
now in the lis

ting of those
wantings and

weakening
s diminish

ing to where
He sat and some

where outside
a bird as yet

indecipher
able as to form

and color

sang.

Two persons? *for* O. B.

Have you
made two per

sons of me:
poet and priest

Can the word
be divided

then as word
and (or)

word But through
the word was

the flesh of
His being

And the word
(the other or samed)

creates a lan

guage of its
own smaller

yet but as I
try in the

love of His
creating

hand.

On his high horse again

the sky's
the route Claim

ing his heroic
stance Saddl

ed in self-
important bus

iness closing
s And I

felt myself
littler than

that looking
up for.

Chassid

His

beard's rhetor
ically gathering

us in for the
flow of ri

vering sounds
through the

clear wants
of his brood

ing eyes to
be boating us

somewhere in
the distant

realms of a
dreamed for

past.

Such stability

Those

heavy wooded
chest of dra

wers Inherited
to be kept a

live by loo
king at Such

stability as
if the past

couldn't be re
moved from

now.

Unlit candle'

s proper

sense for
propriety

slender
ly waxed

as these lif
ting cheru

bic voices
to a light

that's angel
ically im

plied.

"Carrying your heart on your shirt sleeve"

may seem too
heavy there

weighed down
in so much

self-content
ment.

Too large

That

space was
too large to

belong them
selves in

Only possible
with an in

crease of self-
meaning.

Are these plants

but dan
cing figura

tively in
twining a

space-loved

looked.

Over-punctuated

He

over-puncu
ated his

life More stop
s and half-

felt starts
That he began

stuttering-
in truths

Moses-like.

Scholared

He scholar
ed himself

into a care-
fully kept

(Almost meticu
loulsy-

minded way
of self-pro

tective

efficiency.)

Cooled off

for a
plastic sense

reshaping
the depth

in shadow.

Poetry books by David Jaffin

1) **Conformed to Stone,** Abelard-Schuman, New York, 1968, London 1970.

2) **Emptied Spaces,** with an illustration by Jacques Lipschitz, Abelard-Schuman, London 1972.

3) **In the Glass of Winter,** Abelard-Schuman, London 1975, with an illustration by Mordechai Ardon.

4) **As One,** The Elizabeth Press, New Rochelle, N. Y. 1975.

5) **The Half of a Circle,** The Elizabeth Press, New Rochelle, N. Y. 1977.

6) **Space of,** The Elizabeth Press, New Rochelle, N. Y. 1978.

7) **Preceptions,** The Elizabeth Press, New Rochelle, N. Y. 1979.

8) **For the Finger's Want of Sound,** Shearsman Plymouth, England, 1982.

9) **The Density for Color,** Shearsman Plymouth, England, 1982.

10) **Selected Poems,** English/Hebrew, Massada Publishers, Givatyim, Israel, 1982.

11) **The Telling of Time,** Shearsman, Kentisbeare, England, 2000 + Johannis, Lahr, Germany.

12) **That Sense for Meaning,** Shearsman, Kentisbeare, England, 2001 + Johannis, Lahr, Germany.

13) **Into the timeless Deep,** Shearsman, Kentisbeare, England, 2002 + Johannis, Lahr, Germany.

14) **A Birth in Seeing,** Shearsman, Exeter, England, 2003 + Johannis, Lahr, Germany.

15) **Through Lost Silences,** Shearsman, Exeter, England, 2004 + Johannis, Lahr, Germany.